By

Sandra Birchfield Ed. D.

Illustrated by Julie Gentry Ed. S.

Copyright © 2013, 2019 by Sandra Birchfield.

ISBN   Softcover   978-1-950580-31-6

All rights reserved. No part of this book may be reproduced or transmitted in any form or by any means, electronic or mechanical, including photocopying, recording, or by any information storage and retrieval system without express written permission from the author, except in the case of brief quotations embodied in critical reviews and certain other non-commercial uses permitted by copyright law.

This is a true story from memories of my childhood.

Printed in the United States of America.

To order additional copies of this book, contact:
Bookwhip
1-855-339-3589
https://www.bookwhip.com

For my grandchildren Levi,
Benjamin, Josie, and Sophie
May you know a world "Free of Prejudice."

When I was a small girl
Living in my own little world
Things seemed very strange
All the people were prearranged.

Whenever my family would ride the bus
People in the back never raised a fuss
I asked my mommy "Who are those people back there?"
"And why do they have different skin and different hair?

She told me that the world is not a
perfect place
And not all people are of the same race
My Mommy then patted and
held my hand
And said "One day you will understand."

My grandmother lived on Courthouse Hill
We called her Grannie and always will
In her neighborhood children
were always around
Near her home was a community called
"Colored Town."

I asked Grannie about it
and she looked down
And on her face was a terrible frown
She shook her head and I saw a tear
Then she said, "No one should
ever live in fear."

When I was ten a black woman named
Annie came to our home
My Mommy was sick
and could not do her work alone
Annie was not very tall, wore glasses,
and had gray in her hair
She and Mom became good friends
and were a working pair

Annie came to our home often
and was respected
Nothing that we would not do for
ourselves was ever requested.

My parents talked to her a lot,
laughed, and never did offend
An individual because of the color
of their skin

Anyone Entering This Home Will Respect And Will Be Respected

Integration was the law of the land
The black schools were closed
and that was their plan.

People will no longer be prearranged,
separate but equal or just left out
Our Countries' Leaders
are turning things about

Finally children do not have to ask
"Who are those people back there?"

Today my little boy sat with a different friend and they each had different hair and different skin

They rode the school bus, near the front,
in row number four
And have no fear because
"Colored Town" is no more

www.ingramcontent.com/pod-product-compliance
Lightning Source LLC
Chambersburg PA
CBHW050736110526
44591CB00003B/42